Dear Parent,

As your child encounters higher levels of reading difficulty, it is vital that he or she not only follows along with the text, but also understands the meaning of what is being read. Comprehension is often very difficult for young readers, but practice is proven to develop it. Here to help your child with reading comprehension skills are almost 100 pages of questions that accompany short stories and other passages of interest to third-graders.

This colorful workbook features entertaining readings followed by activities that will help your child focus on key skills such as: determining the sequence of events; differentiating between true and false; and identifying the meaning of vocabulary words in context. He or she will practice a range of test-taking formats, too—from multiple choice and sequencing to fill-in-the-blanks and completing charts.

The activities are designed for your child to handle alone, but you can read along and help with any troublesome words, ideas, or questions. Patience is key for reading comprehension. Then together you can check answers at the back of the workbook, and you should always give praise and encouragement for his or her effort. In addition, try to find other ways for your child to practice reading comprehension. You can leave a note that describes what fun activities you and your child will do first, second, and third that day. Later, have your child read a bedtime story to you, and then ask him or her some questions about it. Remember that reading is everywhere, so just use your imagination!

The Library of Congress

Does your local library have a lot of books? There is a library in Washington, D.C., that is one of the largest and most important libraries in the world. It's called the Library of Congress. President John Adams started it in 1800.

The library was first built in the Capitol building and it was meant to be used by Congress. Then in 1814, British troops burned the Capitol building and the library was destroyed. Soon after, Thomas Jefferson offered his own personal book collection to start a new Library of Congress. Jefferson had a very large collection of more than 6,000 books. People liked the idea of being able to go to a library and view books on a wide variety of topics. The Library of Congress still exists in Washington, D.C., today.

Soon, cities around the country started to offer free public libraries where anyone could find and borrow books on nearly any topic. Now, most towns and cities in the country have a free public library. Public libraries are part of the United States government. Every citizen can get a free library card and borrow books. Many students use the library to help them do reports for school. Or they can just read books for fun!

GRADE
3

who   what   where

when   how

FLASH
FORWARD
READING

fact   opinion

Written by **Kathy Furgang**

Illustrations by **Jannie Ho**

FlashKids™
Spark Publishing

Spark Publishing
A Division of Barnes & Noble
120 Fifth Avenue
New York, NY 10011
www.sparknotes.com

ISBN-13: 978-1-4114-0705-3
ISBN-10: 1-4114-0705-9

For more information, please visit *www.flashkidsbooks.com*
Please submit changes or report errors to *www.flashkidsbooks.com/errors*

Printed and bound in the United States

1 3 5 7 9 10 8 6 4 2

Read each question. Circle the correct answer.

1. What happened to the first Library of Congress?

   a. It was shut down by John Adams.

   b. It was burned down by British troops.

   c. The books were stolen by British troops.

   d. The books were added to Thomas Jefferson's personal collection.

2. Who started the Library of Congress?

   a. a president

   b. a soldier

   c. a librarian

   d. a citizen

3. What does the word *offered* in paragraph 2 mean?

   a. stole

   b. burned

   c. gave

   d. read

4. Who gave books to start a new Library of Congress?

   a. George Washington

   b. John Adams

   c. Thomas Jefferson

   d. British soldiers

5. Who can have a library card to a public library today?

   a. adults only

   b. students only

   c. presidents only

   d. any citizen

6. What does the word *public* in paragraph 3 mean?

   a. used by the government only

   b. used by schools only

   c. used by everyone

   d. used by libraries

A Robot Surprise

The strangest thing happened in my town last week. At around lunchtime on Wednesday, a giant robot came walking down the street. It was about the size of some of the tallest buildings in town. People stared up at it in disbelief. It was later spotted in the downtown park. It was stomping on trees and making holes in the ground with its huge feet.

Some people say it came up from under the ocean. Others say it flew here from outer space. Many people were afraid of the robot. One scientist said there was no reason to be afraid unless the robot tried to harm us. The groundskeeper at the park thought the robot had already done harm by making holes in his beautiful lawn.

I liked the robot and thought perhaps it could help us. Many of my friends agreed. My friend Ron thought the robot could help park cars. Judy and Tracy thought it could shovel snow in the winter. I thought the robot could clean windows on tall buildings.

But, just as fast as it appeared, the robot disappeared. He didn't blast off into space or rise into a puff of smoke. He just simply disappeared. Maybe it will return one day. Maybe it won't. Either way, people in my town will never forget what happened around lunchtime last Wednesday afternoon.

Answer the questions below.

1. What is the base word of *disbelief*?

_____

2. Where did some people think the robot came from?

_____

3. Why did the groundskeeper think the robot was harmful?

_____

4. What did the narrator think the robot might be able to do for the townspeople?

_____

5. What happened to the robot at the end of the story?

_____

6. What kind of words are *lunchtime*, *downtown*, and *groundskeeper*?

_____

The Telephone

Life would be very different if you could not pick up the phone and call someone. Today, people easily call each other from different places all over the world. Things were not always this way.

In 1876, an inventor named Alexander Graham Bell tested the first telephone. An inventor's job is to think of ways to make life easier for people. A system called Morse code already worked for sending messages. But it was difficult to use. A message was sent across wires in the form of dots and dashes. Then the message had to be translated into words. Bell thought people should be able to talk to each other over the wires.

The first words to be spoken over the telephone were from Bell to his assistant, Thomas A. Watson. Bell said, "Mr. Watson, come here. I want to see you," into the phone to Watson in the next room. From that point on, communication changed for people all over the world.

It took many years for the telephone to become the tool we know today. First, an operator had to dial the numbers to connect one person to another. Then, people were able to dial phone numbers directly from their telephone. Today, many people have cell phones that they carry with them. The telephone has changed the way people communicate.

Number the events in the correct order according to the reading.

_____ Operators dial phone numbers to connect people.

_____ Alexander Graham Bell tests the first telephone.

_____ People use cell phones to communicate.

_____ People use Morse code to send messages.

_____ People can dial phone numbers directly from their own phones.

The Letter

To whom it may concern,

I shrunk myself. Yes, it is true. It happened last night while I was working on my science experiment. I thought it would be cool to make a shrinking ray to bring in to school on Monday. Little did I know that I would shrink myself by mistake. I had just completed the shrinking ray and was going to test it when it went off in my hands. You see, the phone rang and it scared me, so I pushed the button by mistake. The ray bounced off a mirror and hit me.

Now I am smaller than a fly. In fact, I saw a fly only moments ago. It seemed like a helicopter to me. The sound of its wings was so loud to my shrunken ears. Everything is different now. Pieces of dust are big enough to fit in my fist. My sneakers are like skyscrapers, and my desk is as tall as a mountain.

Right away I knew I needed help. I found a piece of scrap paper on my floor. Then I began looking for a way to write this letter on it. After searching a while I found a tiny pencil shaving on the floor. It feels very heavy to me and it has taken me more than an hour to write this message. Please help. I'm in the corner of the room. Aim the ray at me and help return me to my proper size. Thanks.

Sincerely,
Mike

Complete each sentence.

1. Mike _____ himself by mistake.

2. He was working on a _____ experiment for school.

3. Mike said the shrinking ray went off when the _____ rang.

4. Mike used scrap paper and the shavings from a _____ to write with.

5. It took Mike more than an _____ to write his note.

6. Mike told people they could find him in the _____ of the room.

What Fossils Tell Us

Imagine digging in the ground and finding the bones of an ancient creature that once walked on earth. Scientists find bones and animal imprints in rocks all around the world. A person who studies fossils is called a paleontologist.

Did you know that ancient animal bones, or fossils, give us clues about what earth was like long ago? For example, suppose a scientist finds a fossil of a fish on top of a dry and rocky mountain. What kind of clue does that give us about the past? It tells us that the area was once covered in water. How is that possible? Earth is always changing. Areas that are now dry may have once been covered in lakes or streams. Areas that are now covered in water may have once been dry land.

Scientists also compare fossils from once-living creatures to animals that live today. For example, a dinosaur may have wing bones similar to a kind of bird we know about today. This is a clue that the dinosaur may have moved, flown, or looked similar to some of today's birds.

Fossils are a record of the earth's past. We can look at fossils and tell what has lived on earth. We can also tell what earth's surface was like and how it has changed. Scientists are learning more and more about our planet's past every day.

Read each statement. Write *true* or *false*.

1. Fossils tell us about earth's future.

_____

2. Scientists that study fossils are called paleontologists.

_____

3. Scientists learn about earth by studying fossils.

_____

4. Earth always stays the same, so scientists learn about it by looking at fossils.

_____

5. A dinosaur bone can teach scientists about animals that live today.

_____

6. Areas of earth that are dry may have once been covered in water.

_____

First Haircut

Yesterday my brother Jacob got his first haircut. He is only nine months old. My mom said that his hair was getting so long that many people thought he was a girl.

When Mom told Jacob where we were going, he did not seem to understand. He can't talk yet. He only makes funny noises.

He was fine when we first got to the barbershop. Then my mom put him in the barber seat and he started to fuss a little. Finally, the barber put an apron on him and he started to cry. Mom stood next to him the whole time and held his hand. She sang to him and tried to cheer him up. As soon as the haircut was over, Jacob stopped crying.

Mom told him that each haircut would get easier and easier. She pointed to me and told Jacob that I used to cry when I got my hair cut, too. (I don't remember anything like that.) She said that I cried the first five times I got a haircut, and then it just didn't bother me anymore. Maybe Jacob will feel the same way.

Just before we left, the barber came around to the front of Jacob's stroller. He gave him a small toy star and made him smile. He said he would see him again soon for his next haircut. Jacob smiled and played with the star all the way home.

Read each question. Circle the correct answer.

1. Who was getting the haircut in the story?

   a. the narrator

   b. the narrator's mother

   c. the narrator's sister

   d. the narrator's brother

2. What is the main idea of the story?

   a. Jacob's mom holds his hand and sings to him.

   b. Jacob does not want to get his hair cut.

   c. Jacob cries when an apron is put on him.

   d. Jacob gets a toy star to play with.

3. What kind of character is Jacob's mom?

   a. angry

   b. mean

   c. caring

   d. frightened

4. Which word **best** describes how Jacob feels at the end of the story?

   a. happy

   b. upset

   c. confused

   d. scared

5. What kind of story is this?

   a. nonfiction

   b. fiction

   c. poetry

   d. a play

6. When did Jacob stop crying?

   a. When he first got to the barbershop.

   b. When he sat in the barber chair.

   c. When the apron was put around him.

   d. When his haircut was finished.

Making Crayons

You have probably used hundreds of crayons in your lifetime so far. Have you ever stopped to wonder what crayons are made of? Long ago, the first crayons were made of charcoal and oil. These were hard to use and were not very sturdy. For the last hundred years, the two basic ingredients of crayons have been pigment and wax. Pigment is a powder that gives a crayon its color. Wax is a solid plastic that gives the crayon its look and feel.

Crayons are made in factories with special machines. First, the pigment and wax is combined and heated in large containers until they melt into a liquid. The liquid must be heated to almost 200 degrees Fahrenheit (93 degrees Celsius). The hot liquid is then poured into a mold of crayon-shaped holes. The mold is similar to an ice cube tray. When a liquid is poured into the mold, it hardens to take the shape of the mold. One mold can make more than one thousand crayons. When the liquid has hardened and cooled in the molds, the crayons are pushed out and checked by workers at the factory. They remove any crayons that are broken or imperfect. These crayons can be melted and molded again.

Today, crayon makers can do more than just make a simple crayon. Some crayons glow in the dark, change colors, include glitter, and even wash off surfaces easily.

Complete each sentence. Then write the answers in the puzzle.

Across

1. A powder that gives crayons its color is _____.

2. Crayons can come out of the mold once they have _____.

3. A liquid combination of crayons is poured into a _____.

Down

4. Crayons today are made in a _____.

5. Wax gives crayons their look and _____.

6. One mold can make more than one _____ crayons.

The Spooky House on Charcoal Lane

Yesterday was Halloween. I was really excited about it, except for one thing. My friends and I were just a little afraid of that spooky house on Charcoal Lane. Cindy and Max thought it was haunted. Dave thought it was just an old house. I wasn't quite sure.

My older brother had been to the house last Halloween. When I asked him if it was haunted he just replied, "I'll never tell."

Kids at school said the house was more than 100 years old and was filled with about 50 ghosts. All the shutters on the house were dirty and cracked and several windows were broken. Kids said they could hear the sounds of howls and banging chains coming from the house at night.

Cindy said we shouldn't even go near it on Halloween. She thought we shouldn't risk our lives for some candy. That made sense, but there was a part of me that wanted to find out for sure whether the place was haunted or not. What better day to do it than on Halloween?

So I walked slowly up the sidewalk. Every step I took made my knees shake. Cindy called for me to come back. "Stop! Stop!" she yelled. But I couldn't stop now. I rang the doorbell but nothing happened. So I began to knock. I knocked louder and louder with each bang of my fist. Finally, the door squeaked open. What did I see? I'll never tell.

Answer the questions below.

1. Why were some of the kids afraid of the house on Charcoal Lane?

_____

2. What did the narrator's brother say about what he saw at the house?

_____

3. Who did not want the narrator to go up to the house?

_____

4. How did the narrator feel as he walked up to the door?

_____

5. How did the house look from the outside?

_____

6. Write a few sentences to tell what you think happened when the door opened.

_____

_____

_____

Elephants

People say that an elephant never forgets. That's because an elephant has one of the best memories of any animal or human on earth. The elephant's brain is the largest of any land animal. Elephants play, use tools, and have feelings. They even remember other elephants that have died and they can feel sadness for them.

Elephants live for about 70 years. It takes about 22 months for an elephant to be born. Elephants are usually about 265 pounds when they are born! One of the most interesting parts of an elephant is its trunk. An elephant's trunk is strong enough to carry a log. But it is not only for heavy work. An elephant can pick up small objects with its trunk, such as a single blade of grass. The trunk is even used when an elephant plays. When two elephants greet each other, they might twist their trunks together as a greeting.

In the past, elephants were hunted for their ivory tusks. So many elephants were hunted that the animal became threatened around the world. Today, there are about 400,000 to 600,000 elephants on earth. They are protected from hunting and capture. It is now illegal to hunt an elephant or to buy or trade the animal's ivory tusks.

Read each question. Circle the correct answer.

1. What is the main idea of the first paragraph?

   a. There are 400,000 to 600,000 elephants living today.

   b. Elephants are intelligent animals.

   c. It is illegal to hunt an elephant.

   d. Elephants can lift logs with their trunks.

2. What is **not** a detail of the first paragraph?

   a. Elephants have large brains.

   b. Elephants have good memories.

   c. Elephants live about 70 years.

   d. Elephants can use tools.

3. Where would you **most likely** find a reading like this?

   a. encyclopedia

   b. dictionary

   c. book of poetry

   d. book of short stories

4. Why did people hunt elephants?

   a. for their trunks

   b. for their tusks

   c. for their meat

   d. for their skin

5. Which of these does the reading **not** mention that an elephant can do with its trunk?

   a. pick up logs

   b. pick up a blade of grass

   c. use a paintbrush

   d. twist its trunk with another elephant's

6. Why is it illegal to trade or buy an elephant's tusk?

   a. They are too expensive.

   b. In the past, too many people hunted elephants for their tusks.

   c. Too many people were using the tusks as weapons.

   d. Not enough elephants have tusks anymore.

The Tortoise Race

Yesterday, Tortoise Town had its yearly race. Each year they hold a race to find out who is the fastest tortoise and who is the slowest. The race is very popular. Turtles and tortoises from all over the world come to see or be in the race.

Everyone's favorite fast turtle is Spotted Steve, the Terrapin from the South. He was up against the desert tortoise, Zoomin' Zack. Other racers like Speedy Sam, Fast Freddy, and Quick Quincy were great during the race. They gave Spotted Steve a run for his money! But Spotted Steve came out on top and beat all the others by over a full shell's length. He has won the fastest tortoise race for five years in a row now.

In the slowest tortoise race, the last one to finish is the winner. Barely Moving Bob won this year. Close ahead of him was Late Louie. Barely Moving Bob has been the slowest for over ten years in a row now. He usually falls asleep right at the starting line and wakes up when the others finish. The slow race took over four hours this year, the longest ever.

Overall, the races were very popular this year. Many turtles have fun watching the races. Three hundred seventy-two turtles and tortoises visited the town to watch the races yesterday. Today, the minor league races will be held. The winners there will be able to compete in the pro races next year. The youth league races will end the week as the tiniest tortoises compete for the first time ever.

TORTOISE TOWN RACE

Answer the questions below.

1. Which turtle won the race for the fastest turtle?

_____

2. Which turtle won the race for the slowest turtle?

_____

3. Which races will be held later today?

_____

4. What does Barely Moving Bob usually do at the starting line of a race?

_____

5. How long did the slow race take?

_____

6. What do the other turtles think of the yearly race?

_____

The Sun

Look up at the sky. The only reason you can see what's up there during the day is because the sun is shining. The sun is very important for life on earth. In fact, without the sun, life could not exist here. The sun gives earth its heat and light. But what is the sun?

The sun is a star, just like the stars you see in the night sky. Like all stars, the sun is made of hot gases. It is an average-sized star, too. It only seems so bright because it is closer to us than the other stars we see at night. When we see the sun, there are other stars in the sky also. We can't see these stars during the day because the light from the sun drowns them out. The earth and the other planets travel around the sun while the sun stays in the same place in the solar system.

The sun is 432 thousand miles from one side to the other. The sun is larger than all the planets in the solar system combined. Its surface is 10,000 degrees Fahrenheit. At its center, it is 27 million degrees Fahrenheit!

We're pretty far from the sun. In fact, we're 93 million miles away. Imagine how far away all those other tiny stars are from us!

Read each statement. Write *true* or *false*.

1. The sun is a star.

_____

2. The sun travels around the earth.

_____

3. The sun is much smaller than the earth.

_____

4. The sun is much larger than the earth.

_____

5. There are other stars in the sky during the day that we cannot see.

_____

6. The sun is 93 billion miles away from the earth.

_____

The Discovery

When Lucas and Emily wandered into the woods behind their new home, Emily was less than excited.

"Wait up," said Emily, who was not as fast as Lucas.

"Come on. I'm not going that fast. I want to see what is back here," said Lucas.

Lucas was excited about exploring the woods. They had just moved from the city and had lived in a house with only a small backyard with no trees. But Emily missed their old home and did not enjoy exploring the woods and taking hikes. Then something caught her eye.

"What's that?" she asked and pointed to a brown shape in the trees off in the distance.

"What's what?" asked Lucas. He slowed down a bit.

"I'm not sure," said Emily. She began to walk toward it. Lucas followed.

Soon both of them realized that it was a tree house. It was a secret discovery near their new home! They ran toward it together. They saw that it was very well built and hanging between four strong trees.

From that day on, Emily liked to go into the woods. She brought her favorite book and climbed up the tree to read it in the tree house. Every new friend that Lucas and Emily met loved to visit the tree house, too. Emily did not miss the city anymore.

Number the events in the correct order according to the story.

_____ Emily spotted something through the trees.

_____ Emily does not miss the city anymore.

_____ Lucas and Emily wandered into the woods.

_____ Emily brings books up in the tree house.

_____ Emily could not keep up with Lucas.

_____ Lucas and Emily see a tree house.

Gold Rush!

What would you do if you were walking along a river and saw a sparkle of something in the water? In 1848, a man named James W. Marshall found small pieces of a shiny metal along the American River, near San Francisco, California. When word got out that this shiny metal was gold, things quickly changed in the quiet area.

People thought that if there was one piece of gold in the river, there must be more. A rush for gold began. The newspapers reported the news all around the country. People rushed to the river in California in hopes of finding gold and becoming rich.

Boomtowns developed all around California. A boomtown is an area where towns spring up quickly. Homes, stores, blacksmiths, hotels, and other services popped up almost overnight. People came from across the country, and some even came from across the world.

Many found the gold by panning in the river. Panning means placing a screen in the water to filter out dirt. People hoped to be left with chunks of gold in their pans. So many people came to the area in 1849 that they became known as '49ers. However, there was not enough gold for all the people who came. Soon the boomtowns became ghost towns, or towns with no people. The gold rush was over as quickly as it began.

Match each word or expression to its definition. Write the letter on the line.

1. _____ panning

2. _____ boomtown

3. _____ gold

4. _____ gold rush

5. _____ '49er

6. _____ ghost town

a. time when people rushed to California to look for gold

b. town with no people living in it

c. person who moved to California in 1849

d. filtering out dirt and objects from water

e. area where towns spring up quickly

f. mineral found in the earth's surface

Billy, the Artist

My name is Billy. Last week my mother took me to the art museum near our house. It is one of my favorite places to go. After coming home from the museum I asked my parents if I could have my own paint set. They said I would have to earn the money for the paint set by doing chores around the house.

I did my regular chores, like setting the table for dinner, drying dishes, and folding clothes. Then I did extra chores, like mowing the lawn and picking up leaves and sticks from the yard. Finally, one day after school my mom said she had a surprise for me. She took me into the kitchen, and there on the table was a brand-new paint set waiting for me! She helped me read the instructions and get started on a painting.

For my first painting I decided to paint my family. First, I drew a simple picture of Mom, Dad, and me. When I was done I painted over the drawing with as many paint colors as I could. At dinner I gave the painting to my parents. They were both very happy with it and they hung it on the refrigerator.

Even though I was done with the chores I needed to do to earn the paint set, I guess some chores never end. I had to clean the paintbrushes and clear the table for dinner!

Read each question. Circle the correct answer.

1. What kind of person is Billy?

patient   impatient

2. What did Billy want in the story?

a bike   a paint set

3. How did Billy earn money in the story?

did chores   sold cookies

4. Who had a surprise for Billy one day?

his father   his mother

5. What was the first thing Billy painted?

his family   himself

6. What was the last thing Billy did?

make a painting   clear the table

Your Teeth

You are about to lose yet another tooth. You have been losing them one by one since you were five years old. Did you know that primary teeth, or baby teeth, were already in your gums on the day you were born? At around six or seven months, baby teeth cut through the gums and are visible. All 20 of the primary teeth are usually noticeable by around three years. When your 20 baby teeth fall out one by one, 28 adult teeth replace them. Then, when you are about 20 years old, you grow four more teeth in the back of your mouth called wisdom teeth. That makes a total of 32 adult teeth!

So, what are all these teeth for? Each kind of tooth in your mouth has a different job to do. Your four front top and four front bottom teeth are called incisors. They are used to cut food as you eat it. Next to these teeth are your canine teeth. They are the pointiest teeth in your mouth. They are used to tear into food that may be hard or crunchy. The rest of the teeth in your mouth are used to grind food before you swallow it. The flat teeth in

the far back of your mouth are called molars. They are needed so that you do not choke on your food. All of these teeth together make it possible for you to eat just about anything you want!

Complete each sentence. Then write the answers in the puzzle.

Across

1. The eight teeth used to cut food as you eat it are your _____.

2. A _____ is one of the many flat teeth in the back of your mouth.

3. When you take a bite of food, your _____ teeth can tear the food.

Down

4. The four teeth that grow in the back of your mouth at around 20 years old are _____ teeth.

5. Teeth that grow in after baby teeth fall out are _____ teeth.

6. Baby teeth are also called _____ teeth.

Dargool the Dragon

Dargool the dragon was more than 400 years old. He lived in a cave on the south side of foggy mountains. He had not seen a man dare to go into the mountains for more than 200 years. The last man who had been there warned everyone to stay away from the dragon's cave. Dargool had not harmed the man, but he did blow flames at him. He may have burned a few of his hairs. That was a long time ago.

Now things were changing. The king had ordered his lands to expand to include the foggy mountains. The king did not fear the legend of Dargool. This worried Dargool. He was a peaceful dragon and did not want to hurt anyone, but he liked being alone.

Dargool decided it would be best to find a new home. After days of searching, he found a cave on the far side of a huge tar pit. No creature, man nor beast, could cross it, he thought. It was perfect. He returned to his old cave to start packing. When he got there he saw a member of the king's guard. Dargool breathed fire and scared the man near to death. The man went back and told everyone about Dargool. The king quickly changed his mind about moving into the dragon's lands.

Dargool sat happily in his cave. Now he had two homes: one for the winter months and one for the summer!

Answer the questions below.

1. What is the setting of the story?

_____

2. Is the story written in the present tense or the past tense?

_____

3. Who is making a change to the foggy mountains that will affect Dargool?

_____

4. Why did Dargool want to move from his cave?

_____

5. Where did Dargool find a new home?

_____

6. How does Dargool end up with two homes?

_____

_____

See You Later, Old Calculator

Today you can buy a small, simple calculator in the store for just a few dollars. About 40 years ago, people did not own calculators in their homes. Only mathematicians and scientists used calculators. They were giant machines that cost thousands of dollars. The first calculators in the 1960s were large and clunky. Some weighed more than 30 pounds!

The handheld, or pocket, calculator was not invented until 1970. But it was still very expensive. Most people still used paper and pencil to make calculations. Throughout the 1970s, companies worked to make the calculator smaller, cheaper, and easier to use.

Things sure have changed since the calculator was first introduced. Today, most calculators run on batteries or solar power, which is power from the sun. Calculators can even be found inside tiny cell phones and on computers. When pocket calculators first became cheap and easy to use, students began to use them to do homework. Many teachers feared that students would not learn how to do math by themselves if they used calculators. What do you think?

Answer the questions below.

1. Who used calculators before 1970? _____

2. How much did the first calculators cost? _____

3. What do many students use calculators for?

_____

4. How do many of today's calculators work?

_____

5. How can calculations be made by hand?

_____

6. Do you think students learn how to do math if they use a calculator?
Why or why not?

_____

_____

Music for Sheldon

Sheldon the Squirrel loved music. Of course, everyone knows that it is not easy for a squirrel to listen to music. Sheldon had to listen to the music that humans played. Sometimes he would hang out in the Peabodys' backyard to hear the music from the radio. Other times he would crash the Millers' Friday pool party to listen to some tunes. The warm months of the year were usually pretty easy for Sheldon.

In the winter months, things were much harder. Most people did not go outside during the winter to listen to music. This meant that Sheldon had to sneak into places where humans were to hear music. He once snuck into Mrs. Miller's car to hear the radio as Mrs. Miller drove to work. Then he had to sit inside the cold car all day and wait for her to drive back home. Another time, Sheldon snuck into the Peabodys' house to listen to some CDs. They caught him dancing next to one of the speakers! He almost didn't make it out alive. Sheldon's mother told him how dangerous his music habit was becoming. He promised his mother he would not do it again.

Without music, Sheldon became very sad. Then one day his mother had a surprise for him. It was a radio! She had found it in the trash. The radio had a hand crank so Sheldon could recharge the batteries all by himself. Lucky Sheldon was able to hear music all winter long.

Read each question. Circle the correct answer.

1. What problem does Sheldon have?

  a. He doesn't like music.

  b. His mother does not like music.

  c. He has trouble hearing music in winter.

  d. He has trouble hearing music in summer.

2. Which word **best** describes Sheldon's mother?

  a. angry

  b. concerned

  c. musical

  d. sleepy

3. What time of year does Sheldon probably like best?

  a. spring

  b. summer

  c. fall

  d. winter

4. What is the setting of the story?

  a. in a music store

  b. in a house

  c. throughout a neighborhood

  d. in a bus

5. Who is telling the story?

  a. Sheldon

  b. Sheldon's mother

  c. Mr. Peabody

  d. a narrator

6. How is Sheldon's problem solved?

  a. Sheldon's mother gets him a radio.

  b. Sheldon gives up his love for music.

  c. The Peabodys play music in the winter.

  d. Spring arrives and Sheldon can hear music again.

Clever Chimps

When someone says the word *tool*, you might think of power tools. You might even think of saws, hammers, or screwdrivers. However, a tool is anything that helps you do something. Humans use tools every day. But did you know that animals use tools, too?

Scientist Jane Goodall has studied the behaviors of chimpanzees in the Gombe Stream National Park, in Africa, for many years. She observes the animals in order to learn more about them and how they live. One day in 1960, she observed one of the chimps sitting near a mound of termites. The chimp was placing a twig into the termite hole and then placing the twig into its mouth. It turns out that the chimp was using the twig as a tool to catch and eat termites!

The chimp was using the twig like a fishing pole to catch his food. This seems like a simple thing, but it was quite an amazing discovery. Before this time, people thought that only humans could use tools. As it turned out, animals can do far more than what we thought. Chimps have been seen using twigs, branches, rocks, and leaves to do many different tasks. Some tools help the chimps eat or drink. Others help them clean themselves, and even fight one another.

Answer the questions below.

1. What kind of tools do chimps use?

_____

_____

2. How were chimps discovered using tools?

_____

_____

3. Why do you think using tools shows that chimps are smart?

_____

_____

4. What things can a chimp do with a tool?

_____

_____

5. Where did Jane Goodall do her work with chimpanzees?

_____

_____

6. What would you hope to learn about chimps if you studied them?

_____

_____

The Puppet Show

Every year the local library has a puppet show to help raise money for new books. The kindergarten class always performs the show. But this year there was a big flood in the library. There was a snowstorm with four feet of snow! It was so heavy that part of the roof of the library collapsed. It caused a lot of water and ice damage.

To help raise money to fix the roof, a group of local actors from the Main Street Theater will be putting on the puppet show. Tickets will be more expensive than usual, but they need to be since there is so much damage. The local kindergarten class was upset at first because they thought they would not be able to perform. The actors from Main Street Theater told them they could perform as extras onstage. One or two lucky kids will have small speaking parts.

The show is supposed to be a surprise. But I found out that it will be *The Wizard of Oz*. The kids from the kindergarten class are making some

of the puppets and costumes. They will be getting the help of a mom who is a seamstress. Many children will be playing the parts of trees or flying monkeys from the end of the story.

Everyone is very excited. I think the show will help to raise a lot of money for the library's new roof.

Answer the questions below.

1. Who performs the yearly puppet show at the library?

_____

2. Why will there be another puppet show this year?

_____

3. What show will the actors be performing?

_____

4. What will the money raised at the puppet show be used to buy?

_____

5. Who will be helping the children make puppets and costumes?

_____

6. What parts will the children play in the show?

_____

_____

Origami

Origami is the Asian art of folding paper. The word *origami* comes from the Japanese words *oru* which means "folding," and *kami*, which means "paper." The art is believed to have been brought to Japan from China in the early seventh century.

It was common for people to fold the paper that letters were written on. Over time, people developed ways to fold paper in the shape of animals and other objects. Boats and birds were some of the most common origami shapes. Sometimes boxes were made out of paper and small gifts were placed inside.

Centuries ago, paper was all made by hand and it was much harder to come by. Origami was an art only for the rich. Over time, paper became easier to get and origami became more popular around the world.

Long ago, people passed along the art by word of mouth. There were no written directions about how to fold paper into shapes. Today, there are books that describe how to fold paper into many shapes. Most origami paper starts in the shape of a square. It is colored or patterned on one side and white on the other. Now the amazing art of origami can be learned by anyone with a little patience!

Complete each sentence. Circle the correct answer.

1. Origami is an art from

_____.

   a. the United States

   b. Australia

   c. Asia

2. When making origami, the paper should be_____.

   a. cut

   b. folded

   c. crumpled

3. Most origami paper starts in the shape of a _____.

   a. circle

   b. rectangle

   c. square

4. Today people learn about the art of origami by _____.

   a. word of mouth

   b. reading books

   c. experimenting

5. One of the most common origami shapes is a _____.

   a. bird

   b. bear

   c. box

6. Long ago, many people in China and Japan folded _____ that were written on paper.

   a. stories

   b. letters

   c. instructions

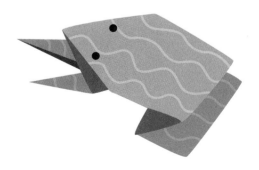

Good Foods

Mom always says it's important for me to try new foods. She says that trying new foods will help me to experience new things I might miss out on. I am not so sure about that. I already like a lot of foods. I enjoy macaroni and cheese. I also like pizza and bagels.

Last night my parents took me out to a restaurant. It was a Japanese restaurant. I had never eaten Japanese food before. Once we got there I was very upset because there was no macaroni and cheese on the menu, and no pizza, either. My parents told me to keep an open mind. They said they would not make me eat anything I didn't like. What if I didn't like anything?

When the food came there were so many different things to look at. My dad said they ordered different foods so that I could have many choices. There was sushi, which is raw fish. There was a plate of dumplings, which are balls of dough with meat inside. There was also fried rice and vegetables. I tried the sushi and did not like it. The dumplings were OK. I tried the fried rice and vegetables. And do you know what? It was very good. I'm glad I tried it and did not miss out! I liked it so much I asked when we were going back to the Japanese restaurant again.

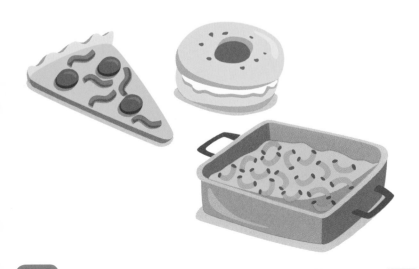

Complete each sentence. Then write the answers in the puzzle.

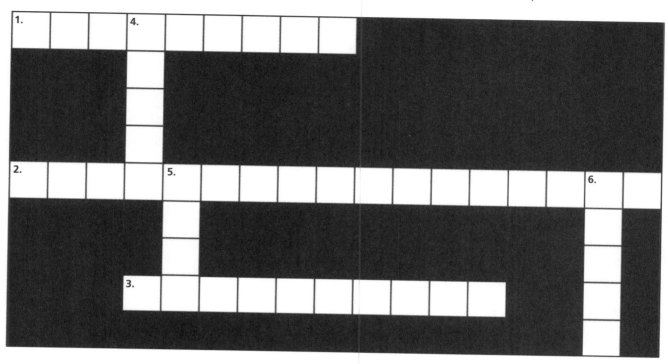

Across

1. Balls of dough with meat inside
are _____.

2. One of the narrator's favorite foods is _____.

3. The narrator tried some fried rice with _____.

Down

4. A flat pie with cheese and sauce is called _____.

5. You can get fried _____ at a Japanese restaurant.

6. A Japanese dish of raw fish is called _____.

Mexico and Corn

In 1521, the Spanish went to Mexico looking for riches. They conquered the land and discovered some wonderful foods, too. They discovered such foods as chocolate, peanuts, vanilla, avocados, and corn.

Corn is probably one of the most important foods in Mexican cooking. The tortilla is a thin pancake made from cornmeal. It is used in Mexican cooking in different ways and for many different purposes. The taco uses a tortilla as a kind of a sandwich. In an enchilada, the tortilla is stuffed and rolled, and then baked. In a quesadilla, the tortilla is filled with foods and then fried.

The traditional way of making tortillas is by pounding cornmeal into dough called *masa*. The masa is then shaped into very thin circles about 8 inches around. The masa can be baked or fried.

Even though Spain conquered Mexico, they did not conquer the Mexican culture. The rich traditions of the country still continue today. The food is among the most memorable parts of Mexican culture, and the tastiest!

Circle the corn with statements that are *true* according to the reading.

Cornmeal is made into a dough called a *vanilla bean*.

A taco is a kind of sandwich that uses a tortilla.

A quesadilla is filled with foods and then fried.

One of the most important foods in Mexican cooking is the peanut.

The Spanish enjoyed many Mexican dishes.

A tortilla is a thin pancake made of oatmeal.

The Crystals

Sam and Jack were having a sleepover in Sam's basement. They found a hole in the basement wall. Inside was a small box. "Open it up," said Sam.

Jack opened the box. A small bag of crystals was inside.

"The crystals are glowing," said Sam. They took the crystals out and held them in their hands. They felt warm. The light they gave off was very bright, but not blinding. Jack squeezed the crystals in his hand and then he started to float. Sam did the same and then he too was floating off the ground!

They went outside and squeezed the crystals in their hands again. This time they floated up high into the sky. The full moon seemed larger and larger as they got higher. It was amazing.

"Hey, come back!" yelled Sam as Jack floated out of sight and into the night sky. Sam didn't know what to do. His friend was gone! Sam dropped his crystals, fell to the ground, and crawled under his sleeping bag to hide. *I'll be in trouble for sure when our parents find out*, he thought. He

worried all night long about his friend. Finally, he fell off to sleep. When he woke up, Jack was in his sleeping bag on the floor next to him. Sam shook Jack awake and asked him about the crystals and his trip into the sky.

"What crystals?" said Jack. Sam scratched his head. What had happened?

Read each question. Circle the correct answer.

1. What kind of story is this?

   a. fiction

   b. nonfiction

   c. poetry

   d. biography

2. What happened when the boys squeezed the crystals?

   a. They glowed.

   b. They rose up into the air.

   c. They fell asleep.

   d. They sank down to the ground.

3. How did Sam feel when his friend disappeared?

   a. glad

   b. amused

   c. scared

   d. angry

4. What happened to Jack when he squeezed the crystals outside?

   a. He glowed.

   b. He floated away and didn't come back.

   c. He was blinded by the light.

   d. He touched the moon.

Answer the questions below.

5. Do you think this kind of story can happen in real life? Why or why not?

_____

_____

6. Why do you think Jack was in his sleeping bag at the end of the story?

_____

_____

Ladybugs

When many people think of bugs, the words *gross* or *yuck* come to mind. But not too many people are sickened by ladybugs. This oval-shaped insect with wings is often thought of as cute. Not only are ladybugs cute, but they also play an important role in keeping pests out of your garden. The favorite food of the ladybug is the *aphid*, which is a tiny insect that sucks the sap from plants. Adult ladybugs can eat more than 50 aphids a day! Without the ladybug, aphids would eat through many garden plants. Aphids can even destroy an entire garden.

Like all insects, ladybugs have three separate body parts. The head has the antennae and eyes. It also has a special part called a *pronotum*, which helps to protect and hide the ladybug's head. The *thorax* is the middle part of the insect's body. Three pairs of legs and wings are attached to this section. The third body part of the ladybug is called the *abdomen*. This section holds many of the body systems for the insect, such as their stomach muscles.

There are nearly 500 different kinds of ladybugs living in the United States, and 5,000 living around the world. The insect is known around the world with different names, including the ladybird, lady beetle, and ladybird beetle. Birds like to eat ladybugs, so this clever insect plays dead to avoid being eaten.

The next time a tiny ladybug lands on you, think about all the ladybug facts you know.

Read each statement. Write *true* or *false*.

1. There are 5,000 kinds of ladybugs in the United States.

_____

2. Aphids eat ladybugs. _____

3. Birds eat ladybugs. _____

4. The legs and wings of the ladybug are attached to its thorax.

_____

5. The ladybug is also known as a lady beetle. _____

6. Ladybugs cause a lot of trouble in a garden. _____

The Farm Boy

Maxwell was 10 years old but he could not read. He could not spell. He did not even know his ABCs. Maxwell lived in the year 1865 and he lived on a farm with his mom and dad. Every day he got up at 4:30 in the morning and did his chores. His first job was to milk the cows. There were 12 of them. When he was done with the cows he fed the chickens, cleaned the barn, washed the wagon, and gathered eggs.

When he gave the eggs to his mom one day he asked why he never went to school. His mom explained that running the farm was more important than going to school. Maxwell wished he could learn new things instead of working on the farm. Most importantly he wanted to learn to read.

One day when Maxwell was done with his chores he went fishing with his friend, David. Maxwell told David about wanting to go to school. David had felt the same way, so his mother was teaching him to read at home. Starting that day, each time the boys went fishing together, David taught Maxwell a little bit more about reading and writing. Soon Maxwell knew his ABCs and could even write his own name.

Maxwell kept practicing his reading for years. When he got older he used his spare time to read books. Maxwell was much happier. He even read about ways to save time doing chores on a farm!

Answer the questions below.

1. Why didn't Maxwell know how to read when he was young?

_____

2. Who taught Maxwell to read? _____

3. How long did it take Maxwell to practice his reading?

_____

4. Which book would Maxwell **most likely** choose to read, a book about fishing or about cooking? Why?

_____

_____

5. Why is reading an important thing to learn?

_____

_____

6. What would you like to learn to do? Why?

_____

_____

How to Make Mini Pizzas

Suppose one day after school you want a tasty treat that's easy to make. Mini pizzas are a great idea for anyone with a grumbling belly. First, toast an English muffin for about one minute. Then take the muffin out of the toaster and put a tablespoon of pizza sauce on each half of the muffin. After that, sprinkle some shredded mozzarella cheese over the pizza sauce. If you like other toppings on your pizza, go right ahead! Pepperoni, sausage, peppers, or mushrooms are all great pizza toppings.

Once your pizza has all the things on it that you like, give it a little sprinkle of Parmesan cheese. Then place it on a cookie sheet and have an adult help you put it in the oven. Bake the mini pizzas at 350 degrees for 20 minutes. Keep an eye on the pizza and take it out of the oven when all the cheese has melted.

You can make as many pizzas as you want at one time. That means that you can have some friends over for a tasty treat after school.

Number the steps in the correct order.

_____ Put a tablespoon of pizza sauce on each half of the muffin.

_____ Bake the pizza at 350 degrees for 20 minutes.

_____ Add extra toppings to your pizza if you like.

_____ Place the pizza on a cookie sheet.

_____ Toast an English muffin for about one minute.

_____ Sprinkle the pizza with Parmesan cheese.

_____ Sprinkle shredded mozzarella over the pizza sauce.

Night at the Lake

Billy was late! He was supposed to meet his best friend, Greg, at Moon Lake just before dark, and it was already dark outside. Greg had called Billy earlier and asked if he could camp at the Lake for one night with him. He said he had found something interesting there that he wanted Billy to see. Greg wouldn't say anything else about it, and now Billy was getting very curious.

When Billy arrived, he didn't see his friend. "Greg," he called out. There was no answer.

Billy wondered if he had come to the right spot, or if perhaps Greg had already left. He started walking around the lake slowly. He wondered to himself what Greg had found that was so interesting. Was it buried treasure, an animal, or perhaps an old dinosaur fossil? His mind raced.

Finally he heard some movement in the bushes. "Greg?" he asked aloud hoping it was Greg and not an animal.

"SURPRISE!" came a huge shout. Suddenly, Greg and all of Billy's friends and family popped out from behind trees and bushes. "HAPPY BIRTHDAY!" they called out. Just then, several cars turned on their headlights to light up a birthday sign and tables set with snacks. It was a surprise birthday party. There was a cake, streamers, and balloons next to the table.

"Wow!" said Billy. "Thanks," he said to everyone. What a fun birthday party it was going to be.

Read each question. Circle the correct answer.

1. Why did Billy go to the lake?

  a. to meet his parents

  b. to meet his friend

  c. to help set up a party

  d. to go fishing

2. How did Billy feel when he got to the lake?

  a. excited

  b. angry

  c. worried

  d. surprised

3. Who did Billy think might be in the bushes?

  a. an animal

  b. a park ranger

  c. his mom

  d. nobody

4. Which word is a compound word?

  a. surprise

  b. suddenly

  c. treasure

  d. birthday

5. Which word does **not** have a suffix?

  a. wondered

  b. interesting

  c. dinosaur

  d. walking

6. Why was Billy happy at the end of the story?

  a. His friends threw him a surprise party.

  b. He found Greg at the lake.

  c. He got to the lake on time.

  d. Greg had found a dinosaur fossil.

The Tale of Cinderella

Once upon a time, a young girl named Cinderella had a mean stepmother and three evil stepsisters. Cinderella waited on them all day. She mopped the floor. She made their meals. She scrubbed the dishes.

Then one day, all the girls in the kingdom were invited to a royal ball. The prince wanted to find a beautiful wife for himself. Of course, Cinderella had to do chores as her stepsisters went to the ball.

Suddenly, a good fairy appeared to Cinderella and turned her ragged dress into a gorgeous gown. She even gave Cinderella a delicate pair of glass slippers to wear.

"Just be back by midnight," said the fairy, "or the spell will wear off!"

When Cinderella arrived at the ball, her stepmother and stepsisters could not believe their eyes. Their servant was the most beautiful girl at the ball. The prince danced with her all night. Cinderella rushed to leave the castle by midnight. On her way out, she lost one of her glass slippers on the castle stairs.

The next day, the prince searched the whole kingdom for the girl who had lost that glass slipper. He wanted that girl to be his bride. And who do you think was the only person who fit into that slipper? Cinderella! One day she was a servant to her evil stepmother. The next day she was a beautiful princess living in a castle. Cinderella and the prince lived happily ever after.

Match each character to his or her description. Write the letter on the line.

1. _____ looking for a beautiful bride

2. _____ cleans the house all day

3. _____ went to the ball but did
        not get chosen by the prince

4. _____ has all her meals made for her

5. _____ makes a gown and slippers appear

a. Cinderella

b. stepmother

c. stepsisters

d. the prince

e. fairy

Some characters in the story are good and some are evil.
Place each character in the column where he or she belongs.

Good	Evil

Summer vs. Winter

My favorite season is summer. Why? During summer there are more hours of daylight and the weather is warmer than it is in any other season! I spend most of my summer days at the pool, which is just about the best place anyone can wish to be on a summer day. At night I go to bed just as it is getting dark outside.

I also like summer because there is no school. School ends in June and it does not start again until the beginning of September. I'm glad there is no school during summer. It is just too hot!

Winter is my least favorite season. I like snow, but it doesn't snow enough near my house for me to make a lot of snowmen. Winter has very short days, and it is dark by about 5:00 PM. There are no leaves on the trees, so plants do not look as pretty as they do in summer. My sister loves winter, so I know there are some fun things about it. I just happen to love the summertime.

Read each statement. Write *fact* or *opinion*.

1. My favorite season is summer. _____

2. There are more hours of daylight and the weather is warmer in summer.

_____

3. School ends in June and it does not start again until the beginning
of September. _____

4. The winter has very short days, and it is dark by 5:00 PM. _____

5. There are no leaves on the trees, so plants do not look as pretty as they do
in summer. _____

6. Winter is my least favorite season. _____

Penelope Rabbit

Penelope Rabbit had a problem. She had too much food. This was an unusual problem for a little rabbit like Penelope. Normally it takes Penelope all day to munch away at garden after garden and fill her belly with food.

This year, in addition to the regular gardens in the neighborhood, she found a new source of food. A new food market had opened up in town. They had their own small farm, too. Many of the people bought food from the market and picked less from their own gardens. Penelope Rabbit ate at the small gardens every day and then went to the small farm for more. The market also had extra food that it did not sell. The leftover food was thrown away. Penelope Rabbit took all that extra food back to her rabbit hole.

Soon Penelope Rabbit realized she had way too much food. She did not want all the food to go to waste so she decided to have a party. She gathered all her extra carrots, peas, tomatoes, celery, broccoli, peppers, cucumbers, and spices. She would cook a giant soup for the town. She made signs, wrote letters, and even made a phone call or two to spread the word.

When the day of the party finally came, Penelope Rabbit stood in the middle of the park, serving a delicious vegetable soup. Everyone loved it and not a single vegetable or a drop of soup was wasted.

Write an effect to each cause on the chart.

Cause	Effect
1. There is a new market in town.	
2. Penelope collects extra food from neighbors.	
3. The new market throws out its extra food.	
4. Penelope does not want her food to go to waste.	
5. Penelope sends out invitations.	
6. Penelope makes a vegetable soup.	

Dalmatians

Have you ever seen a Dalmatian running through the park? Dalmatians are those pretty white dogs with black spots all over them. People often think of Dalmatians when they think of fire trucks. That's because Dalmatians were once used to chase rats out of London fire stations. They were also trained to run alongside horse-drawn fire wagons to help the horses find their way in the city streets. Many fire stations kept the dog as a pet for this reason. Today some fire stations keep Dalmatians as pets just for fun.

It is best to keep a Dalmatian busy because these dogs are very active and can become easily bored. Dalmatians need a lot of exercise and do not get tired easily, so they need a lot of space to run around.

Dalmatian puppies are born white and grow their spots later. They usually grow either black or brown spots, but some grow both colors. Most full-grown Dalmatians weigh about 40 to 70 pounds. Female Dalmatians are usually smaller, but some males have grown as large as 90 pounds!

Read each statement. Write *true* or *false*.

1. Most Dalmatians are black with white spots. _____

2. Female Dalmatians grow bigger than males. _____

3. Some fire stations today keep Dalmatians as pets. _____

4. Dalmatian puppies are born with their spots. _____

5. Most Dalmatians are lazy and like to relax all day. _____

6. Dalmatians were once used to chase rats out of fire stations.

_____

Rebecca Red Hood

Rebecca Red Hood had to visit her grandmother who was sick with a runny nose. She had received an e-mail from Grandma asking if she could please bring some hot, spicy soup over to her. Rebecca got right to work making the soup and preparing some other goodies to bring. She put everything in a big brown bag and headed out into the woods. She wore, as always, her long red sweatshirt with the big hood. It was her favorite.

On the way to her grandmother's house a wolf was tracking her every move. The wolf knew all about Rebecca and her sick grandmother. He beat her to the house and tricked Rebecca's grandmother into letting him in by asking to read her electric meter. Once inside he locked Grandma in the basement. The wolf then dressed up in Grandma's clothes and got into her bed. When Rebecca came to the house with the soup he would pounce on her and eat her up. Then he would eat the soup, too!

Luckily, Grandma's cell phone was with her in the basement. She used it to send a text message to Rebecca. She warned Rebecca about the wolf's evil plans. As Rebecca came in the door she spilled the hot soup all over the wolf. He ran away frightened, burned, scared, and wet.

Rebecca felt bad that she did not have any soup for her grandmother. Together they ordered takeout food and chatted while surfing the web. Grandma was already feeling better.

Number the events in the correct order according to the story.

_____ Grandma sent Rebecca a text message.

_____ Rebecca received an e-mail from Grandma.

_____ Rebecca put on her hooded sweatshirt.

_____ Rebecca threw the hot soup on the wolf.

_____ Rebecca cooked some soup.

_____ Rebecca and Grandma ordered takeout food.

_____ The wolf put Grandma in the basement.

How to Bake an Apple Pie

Ingredients:

$\frac{1}{3}$ cup sugar

$\frac{1}{4}$ cup flour

$\frac{1}{2}$ teaspoon nutmeg

$\frac{1}{2}$ teaspoon cinnamon

8 medium-sized apples

2 tablespoons butter

store-bought piecrust with top and bottom

Heat the oven to 425 degrees. Peel, core, and slice the apples with help from an adult. Mix the sugar, flour, and nutmeg in a large bowl. Stir the ingredients so that they are evenly mixed. Pour in the apples and stir them so that the sugar and flour mixture covers all of the apple pieces as evenly as possible.

Make sure you have a piecrust with a top and bottom section. Pour the apple mixture into the bottom crust. Then place small pieces of butter on the apple mixture. Cover the mixture with the top of the piecrust. Seal the edges and cut small slits on the top of the pie. Bake the pie for 50 minutes or until juice comes through the slits in the crust.

Number the steps in the correct order.

_____ Mix the apples with the flour mixture.

_____ Heat the oven to 425 degrees.

_____ Mix the flour, sugar, and nutmeg.

_____ Bake the pie for 50 minutes.

_____ Seal the edges of the piecrusts.

_____ Peel, core, and slice the apples.

_____ Pour the apples into the crust.

The Ant and the Grasshopper

One fine summer day, a silly grasshopper played and relaxed the day away. "What a beautiful day," he said to some ants passing by him. Then he noticed that the ants were all hauling seeds and other foods on their backs. "What are you doing?" he asked them.

"We're collecting food for the winter," said one of the ants. "You should do the same. Haven't you gathered any food for winter?"

"Winter?" laughed the grasshopper. "It's the middle of summer! There will be plenty of time to collect food. Now is the time when we should enjoy the warm days." So all summer long the grasshopper played in the fields and swam in the lake.

Soon fall came and the grasshopper was still wasting the days away. "Don't you want to be prepared for winter?" asked the ant. "You will not have any food left if you do not hurry!"

The grasshopper looked around. The trees were bare. The summer fruits and seeds were gone from the plants. "Hmm," he said. "Maybe you are right." The grasshopper could not find any food to save for winter.

Once winter came, the grasshopper was near starving. He had wasted the summer and fall away. He went to the ants to beg for food. They laughed in his face and sent him on his way.

So, what is the moral of this fine fable? Plan ahead and be prepared! Tomorrow will be here before you know it.

Read each question. Circle the correct answer.

1. Which word in paragraph 1 means *carrying*?

a. working

b. collecting

c. hauling

d. playing

2. Which word in paragraph 2 means the same as *gathering*?

a. walked

b. collecting

c. starving

d. taught

3. Which word means the same as *prepared* in paragraph 4?

a. strong

b. not strong

c. ready

d. not ready

4. Which word means the same as *moral* in the last paragraph?

a. fable

b. lesson

c. tale

d. goodness

5. Which word in paragraph 6 has the closest meaning to *hungry*?

a. starving

b. prepared

c. relaxed

d. swam

6. Which word has the closest meaning to *beg* in paragraph 6?

a. ask

b. write

c. talk

d. jump

How We Hear Sound

What was that sound? All the sounds you hear all day are made in the same way. Sound is made by vibrations, or trembles. Slam your hand down on the table. When your hand hits the table, the air around the table vibrates. The vibrations move out in waves through the air. These waves are called sound waves. The sound waves continue to move through the air and into your ear. Inside your ear is a small body part called an eardrum. When the waves reach your eardrum, the eardrum vibrates. Then these vibrations are turned into nerve impulses that are sent to your brain. Your brain then recognizes the nerve signals as different sounds.

Different vibrations are heard in different ways. For example, volume is how loud or soft a sound is. A whisper is a soft sound, and a shout is a loud sound. Pitch is how high or low a sound is. A chirping bird makes a high-pitched sound. A lion's roar makes a low-pitched sound. If you play a musical instrument you can make both high-pitched and low-pitched sounds. Music is a combination of different sounds. A flute usually makes a softer sound than a trumpet. Both instruments can make high pitches or low pitches.

Circle the ears with *nouns*.

sound

vibrate

music

vibration

high

eardrum

loud

whisper

soft

volume

low

brain

pitch

Paul Bunyan

This is the story of the world's biggest, strongest man. On the day Paul Bunyan was born, twelve storks had to carry him home to his mother. She could not believe her eyes when she saw him! There were no baby clothes big enough for him, so his mother had to put him in his father's clothes. She fed him 100 baby bottles a day.

When Paul grew older, he became one of the strongest men in the world. So he did the job a strong man could do best. He became a logger. A logger cuts down trees in the woods and helps to carry them out. Paul joined a crew of loggers who worked in the woods all day.

Logging made Paul work up a big appetite. Paul's favorite food was pancakes, so the crew's cooks made him about 400 pancakes each morning. The food gave Paul energy to keep on logging.

One fine morning, the cooks did not have enough eggs to make Paul's pancakes. Paul was so upset that he walked off with his giant ax trailing behind him. The ax made a giant gash in the ground. Of course, this was no ordinary gash because Paul Bunyan made it. It was the biggest gash ever made. Today you can still see the gash Paul made in the ground. We call it the Grand Canyon.

Read each statement. Write *true* or *false*.

1. Twelve storks carried Paul Bunyan home to his mother. _____

2. Paul wore his mother's clothes when he was a baby. _____

3. Paul became a reporter when he grew up. _____

4. Cooks made Paul 400 pancakes every morning. _____

5. Paul dragged his ax behind him and made a gash in the ground.

_____

6. The gash Paul made became known as Lake Michigan. _____

Spiders: Don't Call Them Insects

Many people think of spiders as insects. But they're not! Spiders are actually a class of animals called arachnids. Scorpions, ticks, mites, and spiders are all arachnids.

The main difference between an insect and a spider is the number of legs on each animal. All insects have six legs. Spiders have eight legs. Another difference between an insect and a spider is the body of each animal. An insect has three body parts: the head, the abdomen, which is the stomach, and the thorax, which is the part between the head and stomach. The spider only has only two body parts, the head and the abdomen, or stomach.

Just try to find an insect that can make a web. You won't find one. Spiders are special because most of them can make webs. Spiders make their silky webs from a material in their abdomens. Spiderwebs are used for getting from place to place and for catching insects. Many insects fly or climb into the web and get stuck there. The spider can then eat an insect right away, or wrap it in a silky cocoon to eat it later.

A spider catches its prey by using its sharp fangs to inject poison into its victim. But don't worry about getting a spider bite. Most spiders do not bite humans. They are actually a help to humans. They eat harmful insects that might bite people or harm a plant or garden.

Read each statement. Write *true* or *false*.

1. Spiders are arachnids.

_____

2. Spiders make webs from a sticky material in their mouths.

_____

3. Most spiders are not harmful to people.

_____

4. Spiders have a head, thorax, and abdomen.

_____

Answer the questions below.

5. How are spiders different from insects?

_____

_____

6. How are spiders helpful to people?

_____

_____

Rosa Parks

Can one person make a difference? You bet! One person made a big difference in gaining rights for African Americans. On December 1, 1955, an Alabama woman named Rosa Parks was coming home from work on a bus. She refused to give her seat to a white man. She was arrested and brought to jail for what she did. It was the law at the time that African Americans had to ride in the backs of city buses. They did not have the same rights as white Americans. If a white person needed a seat on the bus, an African American had to give up their seat for them. Ms. Parks thought that the law was unfair. So she did not give up her seat. She knew her actions would bring a lot of attention to the problem of unfair laws for African Americans. She was right.

Many people agreed with what Ms. Parks did. They decided to start a boycott of the Montgomery, Alabama, city buses. A boycott is when people avoid using something. Dr. Martin Luther King, Jr., helped organize the boycott. Instead of paying to ride on the buses, they decided to walk or share car rides until the bus company changed their laws. More than a year later, the bus company did change their laws. The boycott brought attention to the unfair bus law and many other laws that kept African Americans from having the same rights as other Americans.

Rosa Parks

Read each question. Circle the correct answer.

1. Where did Rosa Parks live in 1955?

Washington, D.C.   **Montgomery, Alabama**

2. Why did Rosa Parks get arrested?

She refused to give up her seat on a bus.   **She refused to pay her bus fare.**

3. What happens in a boycott?

People refuse to do or buy something.   **People write letters to complain about something.**

4. Who helped to spread the word about the unfair laws toward African Americans?

the mayor of Montgomery   **Martin Luther King, Jr.**

5. How did people get around during the bus boycott?

They walked or shared car rides.   **They rode buses from a different company.**

6. How long did the bus boycott last?

one year

one week

Maddie, Expert Babysitter

Since she was a little girl, Maddie Knowles wanted nothing more than to be a babysitter. Now she was happy about going on her first babysitting job. Her older sister, Sophie, had been the neighborhood babysitter for years. Now Sophie had a job at the mall. Sophie told the families that she worked for to call her little sister, Maddie, if they wanted a new babysitter.

Sophie taught Maddie everything she knew about babysitting. She told her about all the kids she would have to care for and what they were like. Maddie even took a babysitting course to learn first aid and what to do in other emergencies.

Maddie was very nervous about her first job. She had to take care of the eight-month-old Largo twins. Maddie had heard that babies can be a lot of work. And there were two of them! But she showed up at the door at 8:00 PM, just like she was supposed to. The parents had to make it to an 8:45 movie. They gave Maddie their cell phone number in case of emergencies. Maddie looked around the house expecting to see the twins crawling on the floor or crying for their bottles. But they were already asleep!

Maddie was relieved to sit on the couch and read a book. But what if the twins wake up, she thought? Maddie panicked again. She wondered if babysitting would be harder than she dreamed about as a little girl.

Answer the questions below.

1. Who did Maddie learn about babysitting from? _____

2. What did Maddie's babysitting course teach her?

_____

3. Who did Maddie have to babysit for on her first day? _____

4. How did Maddie feel as she walked up to the house? _____

5. What happened inside the house that changed the way Maddie felt?

_____

_____

6. Explain how Maddie felt in the last paragraph and why.

_____

_____

The Pony Express

Each day you go to your mailbox and get the mail from the box. Did you ever wonder how the U.S. Postal Service got its start? Back at the time of the American Revolution, messages were delivered on foot or on horseback. The United States kept getting bigger and bigger. Mail had to be delivered across the growing country. By 1860, California needed a good system for getting mail. A system called the Pony Express was developed. It covered a distance of 1,800 miles, from St. Joseph, Missouri, to Sacramento, California. Horse riders constantly took messages back and forth on the trail. The trail went through parts of Missouri, Kansas, Nebraska, Colorado, Wyoming, Utah, Nevada, and California. Riders would travel about 75 to 100 miles per day. It took about 10 days for mail to make it from one end of the trail to the other.

United States mail was later delivered on stagecoaches, and even on steamboats. Then trains, cars, and planes were used. Each time a new kind of transportation came to the United States, the Postal Service used it to deliver mail.

Today, the United States Postal Service delivers hundreds of millions of messages each day. It delivers to more than 140 million homes and businesses throughout the country. Unlike the Pony Express, most mail today is delivered in just a few days.

Number each transportation method used by the Postal Service in the order that it was used.

_____ by stagecoach or steamboat

_____ by foot or on horseback

_____ by car, train, or plane

Answer the questions below.

4. What was the Pony Express? _____

_____

5. Why was it used? _____

_____

6. Where did it pass through? _____

_____

How to Pick the Perfect Present

Jack sat with his mother in the car. "I know what I want to buy Amy," he said. He had been looking forward to shopping for Amy's present all year. Amy and Jack had been best friends since preschool. They always liked the same things. Jack's favorite things to play with were cars, so he knew that's what he wanted to buy Amy for her birthday.

"Jack," said his mom. "You really should think about Amy when you shop, not yourself."

"But Amy loves everything I do," said Jack. "Whatever I pick for myself is the perfect present for Amy."

"When you pick the perfect present for someone, you can't think of yourself. You have to think about the person you're buying the gift for," said his mom.

Maybe Mom was right, thought Jack. Lately Amy has wanted Jack to paint pictures with her. He would try to get her to keep playing with cars, but she was just doing it to make him happy. Was he just thinking about himself? He didn't mean to. He thought again about his friend. Maybe she should get something that would be special to her.

"OK," said Jack to his mom. "Let's go to that art supply store over there instead of the toy store. I think paintbrushes might be the perfect present for her."

"That sounds like a good idea," said Jack's mom.

Write an effect to each cause on the chart.

Cause	Effect
1. Amy's birthday is coming up.	
2. Jack thinks he and Amy have the same likes and interests.	
3. Jack's mother tells him to think about Amy before deciding on a gift.	
4. Jack changes his mind about what to buy.	

Answer the questions below.

5. How long have Jack and Amy been friends?

_____

6. What does Jack's mother think about his decision at the end of the story?

_____

_____

What Should You Do with That Bottle?

You buy a plastic drink bottle from a deli. You enjoy it on a hot summer day. What should you do with the bottle once you are finished with it? If you throw it away you will be adding to our landfills. Landfills are a place where garbage is brought. But landfills can become full. The garbage there takes a very long time to rot. Some of the garbage in landfills will not rot away at all.

Plastic is one material that will not rot away. That's why it is a good idea to recycle the plastic bottle. Recycling is a process that turns an old thing into something new again. If you recycle the bottle, it will be used to make more plastic products. This is a good idea because it cuts down on trash. It will be made into new plastic. The new plastic can then be used to make more bottles or other plastic items.

Recycling is often just as easy as throwing something in a garbage can. Many stores and public places have recycling bins right next to the garbage cans. Just check to see what can be recycled in the bins. Often glass and plastic items can be placed together. They are then collected and separated before they go through the recycling process.

So when you look at that plastic bottle that you just used, think about the best thing to do with it. Recycle it!

Complete the Venn diagram. Compare throwing an item away with recycling it. One is done for you.

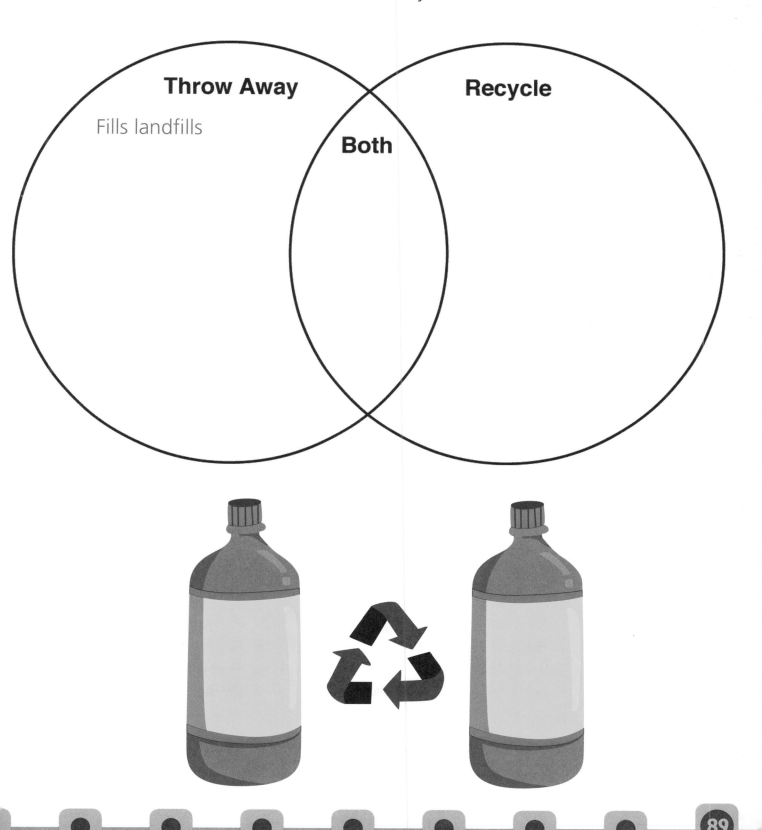

Throw Away

Fills landfills

Both

Recycle

Ants at a Picnic

"Places, everyone!" yelled Andre. The ants quickly lined up and stood at attention. Andre was the leader of this ant party. They were preparing to attack the first spring picnic in Washington Park. They were excited to finally be getting some fresh, picnic food after a long winter.

"Why are we stopping at this garbage can?" asked Abby. "I thought the best picnic food was in the picnic baskets." Abby had been at picnics before. Strawberries were her favorite food and she was hoping to find some today.

Andre explained his plan. "We're only here to hide," he said. "Everyone expects to see ants at a garbage can. They won't stomp on us or try to get rid of us here. Then, when the picnic starts, we'll move in when they least expect it."

Three jolly people sat down for a picnic. They laughed and chatted and took out plenty of food from their basket. "Now!" yelled Andre. The ants ran from the garbage can right over to the picnic basket without stopping. A woman screamed. A child shouted. A man stomped his fist down on the blanket ten times. The ants rushed as fast as they could. Abby dug into a plate of strawberries! Four of her friends helped her carry a strawberry piece over their heads. Then the man's fist came closer and closer to them.

"Retreat!" yelled Andre. The ants ran back to the garbage can as quickly as they could. Picnic season had begun!

Number the events in the correct order according to the story.

_____ Andre tells the ants to run toward the picnic.

_____ The ants gather food and run away.

_____ The ants have a long winter.

_____ Andre gathers the ants near a garbage can.

_____ Some people set down a picnic basket and start eating.

_____ Abby asks why they are not gathering near a picnic basket.

_____ The ants scare the people at the picnic.

The World's Tallest Mountain

The world's tallest mountain is Mount Everest, located between Nepal and China. The mountain is more than 29,000 feet from sea level to its highest peak. It is part of the Himalaya mountain range in Asia.

Many people have tried to climb Mount Everest. Because climbing supplies and the ability to forecast weather improves all the time, more and more people are successful. There have been more than 3,000 people who have made it to the top of the mountain. However, more than 200 have died trying to get there.

Climbing the mountain is dangerous for several reasons. The air gets very thin when climbers reach high up the mountain. It becomes hard to breathe. Only experts can do the difficult rock climbing needed along parts of the trail. There are also plenty of loose rocks. Climbers can slip and fall thousands of feet. Long stretches of the trail have snow several feet deep. Avalanches, which are large pieces of snow that slide down a mountain, are a danger just about anywhere on the mountain. Climbers have tried to reach the top of the mountain since 1921. The first successful climbers did not make it to the top until 1953.

Mount Everest

Today climbers have much better supplies to stay safe and keep warm. Many travel in larger groups for safety. All these things together make climbing the world's tallest mountain possible.

Read each statement. Write *true* or *false*.

1. Mount Everest is the world's second tallest mountain.

_____

2. Only three people have died trying to climb Mount Everest.

_____

3. The air gets thinner as people climb the mountain.

_____

4. There are just a few places on the mountain where an avalanche is possible.

_____

5. The first successful climbers made it to the top of the mountain in 1921.

_____

6. Climbers have better equipment today than they did in 1953.

_____

Answer Key

Answers to some of the pages may vary.

Page 5
1. b
2. a
3. c
4. c
5. d
6. c

Page 7
1. belief
2. from under the ocean or from outer space
3. The robot ruined the lawn that the groundskeeper cares for.
4. wash the windows on tall buildings
5. It disappeared.
6. compound words

Page 9
3 Operators dial phone numbers to connect people.
2 Alexander Graham Bell tests the first telephone.
5 People use cell phones to communicate.
1 People use Morse code to send messages.
4 People can dial phone numbers directly from their own phones.

Page 11
1. shrunk
2. science
3. phone
4. pencil
5. hour
6. corner

Page 13
1. false
2. true
3. true
4. false
5. true
6. true

Page 15
1. d
2. b
3. c
4. a
5. b
6. d

Page 17

Page 19
1. They thought it was haunted.
2. "I'll never tell."
3. Cindy
4. nervous
5. It looked like a haunted house with broken windows and shutters.
6. Answers may vary.

Page 21
1. b
2. c
3. a
4. b
5. c
6. b

Page 23
1. Spotted Steve
2. Barely Moving Bob
3. the minor league races
4. falls asleep
5. 4 hours
6. They think the races are fun to watch.

Page 25
1. true
2. false
3. false
4. true
5. true
6. false

Page 27
3 Emily spotted something through the trees.
6 Emily does not miss the city anymore.
1 Lucas and Emily wandered into the woods.
5 Emily brings books up in the tree house.
2 Emily could not keep up with Lucas.
4 Lucas and Emily see a tree house.

Page 29
1. d
2. e
3. f
4. a
5. c
6. b

Page 31
1. patient
2. a paint set
3. did chores
4. his mother
5. his family
6. clear the table

Page 33

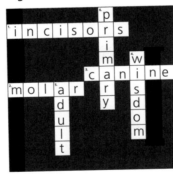

Page 35
1. a cave in the foggy mountains
2. past tense
3. the king
4. He wants to be alone and people will be moving to the mountains.
5. on the far end of a tar pit
6. The king changed his mind about moving to the mountains after Dargool scared someone from his guard. Dargool had already found a new home, so he now had two of them.

Page 37
1. mathematicians and scientists
2. thousands of dollars
3. to do math homework
4. with batteries or solar power
5. with paper and pencil
6. Answers may vary.

Page 39
1. c
2. b
3. b
4. c
5. d
6. a

Page 41
1. twigs, branches, rocks, leaves
2. Jane Goodall observed them using twigs to get termites out of a hole.
3. Answers may vary.
4. find food, clean themselves, or fight
5. Gombe Stream National Park in Africa
6. Answers may vary.

Page 43
1. the kindergarten class
2. the library was damaged by a storm and they need money for repairs
3. *The Wizard of Oz*
4. a new roof for the library
5. a mom who is a seamstress
6. trees and flying monkeys

Page 45
1. c
2. b
3. c
4. b
5. a
6. b

Page 47

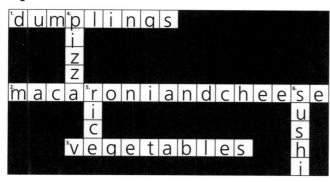

Crossword answers:
- 1 (Across): dumplings
- 1 (Down): pizza
- 2 (Across): macaroniandcheese
- 5 (Down): rice
- 6 (Down): sushi
- 3 (Across): vegetables

Page 49

Circled statements:

A taco is a kind of sandwich that uses a tortilla.

A quesadilla is filled with foods and then fried.

The Spanish enjoyed many Mexican dishes.

Page 51

1. a
2. b
3. c
4. b
5. Possible answer: No, because magical things do not happen in real life.
6. Possible answer: He was actually dreaming about the crystals.

Page 53

1. false
2. false
3. true
4. true
5. true
6. false

Page 55

1. He had to work on his parents' farm all day.
2. his friend, David
3. many years
4. He might choose a book about fishing because he likes to fish.
5. Possible answer: Reading helps people to learn new things.
6. Answers may vary.

Page 57

2 Put a tablespoon of pizza sauce on each half of the muffin.

7 Bake the pizza at 350 degrees for 20 minutes.

4 Add extra toppings to your pizza if you like.

6 Place the pizza on a cookie sheet.

1 Toast an English muffin for about one minute.

5 Sprinkle the pizza with Parmesan cheese.

3 Sprinkle shredded mozzarella over the pizza sauce.

Page 59

1. b
2. c
3. a
4. d
5. c
6. a

Page 61

1. d
2. a
3. c
4. b
5. e

"Good" characters: Cinderella, fairy, prince

"Evil" characters: stepmother, stepsisters

Page 63

1. opinion
2. fact
3. fact
4. fact
5. opinion
6. opinion

Page 65

1. People buy vegetables at the market instead of using their own gardens.
2. She has too much food.
3. Penelope collects the extra food.
4. Penelope decides to have a party.
5. Lots of people come to the party.
6. She uses the extra vegetables.

Page 67

1. false
2. false
3. true
4. false
5. false
6. true

Page 69

5 Grandma sent Rebecca a text message.

1 Rebecca received an e-mail from Grandma.

3 Rebecca put on her hooded sweatshirt.

6 Rebecca threw the hot soup on the wolf.

2 Rebecca cooked some soup.

7 Rebecca and Grandma ordered takeout food.

4 The wolf put Grandma in the basement.

Page 71

4 Mix the apples with the flour mixture.

1 Heat the oven to 425 degrees.

3 Mix the flour, sugar, and nutmeg.

7 Bake the pie for 50 minutes.

6 Seal the edges of the piecrusts.

2 Peel, core, and slice the apples.

5 Pour the apples into the crust.

Page 73

1. c
2. b
3. c
4. b
5. a
6. a

Page 75

Circled words:

sound, music, eardrum, vibration, whisper, brain, pitch, volume

Page 77

1. true
2. false
3. false
4. true
5. true
6. false

Page 79

1. true
2. false
3. true
4. false
5. Spiders have 8 legs and 2 body parts. Insects have 6 legs and 3 body parts.
6. Spiders eat insects and other animals that can bite people and harm their plants and gardens.

Page 81

1. Montgomery, Alabama
2. She refused to give up her seat on a bus.
3. People refuse to do or buy something.
4. Martin Luther King, Jr.
5. They walked or shared car rides.
6. one year

Page 83

1. her sister, Sophie
2. first aid and what to do in emergencies
3. the eight-month-old Largo twins
4. nervous
5. The twins were already asleep.
6. She was nervous that she wouldn't know what to do with the twins if they woke up.

Page 85

2 by stagecoach or steamboat

1 by foot or on horseback

3 by car, train, or plane

4. The Pony Express was a system of carrying mail halfway across the country by horseback.
5. A good system was needed to carry mail long distances.
6. Missouri, Kansas, Nebraska, Colorado, Wyoming, Utah, Nevada, and California

Page 87

1. Jack and his mom go out to buy a present for her.
2. Jack wants to buy Amy a car for her birthday.
3. Jack remembers that Amy likes to paint.
4. Jack decides to buy paintbrushes for Amy.
5. since preschool
6. She thinks he made a good decision.

Page 89

Throw Away

Fills landfills
Cannot be used again

Recycle

Does not use landfills
Items are made into new things
Cuts down on garbage

Both

Item cannot be used again for original purpose

Page 91

<u>5</u> Andre tells the ants to run toward the picnic.
<u>7</u> The ants gather food and run away.
<u>1</u> The ants have a long winter.
<u>2</u> Andre gathers the ants near a garbage can.
<u>4</u> Some people set down a picnic basket and start eating.
<u>3</u> Abby asks why they are not gathering near a picnic basket.
<u>6</u> The ants scare the people at the picnic.

Page 93

1. false
2. false
3. true
4. false
5. false
6. true